Sunk in Your Shipwreck

Sunk in Your Shipwreck

A Palmer Stammering

JACOB RIYEFF

RESOURCE *Publications* · Eugene, Oregon

SUNK IN YOUR SHIPWRECK
A Palmer Stammering

Resource Publications
An Imprint of Wipf and Stock Publishers
199 W. 8th Ave., Suite 3
Eugene, OR 97401

www.wipfandstock.com

PAPERBACK ISBN: 978-1-5326-6245-4
HARDCOVER ISBN: 978-1-5326-6246-1
EBOOK ISBN: 978-1-5326-6247-8

Manufactured in the U.S.A.   09/07/18

for David, Kim, and Paul Riyeff

Contents

Acknowledgments

POEMS IN THIS COLLECTION have appeared in the following laudable and gracious journals: *Marquette University Literary Review, Poetry Quarterly, Bijou Poetry Review, Foliate Oak, Schuylkill Valley Journal, Vine Leaves, Three Line Poems, Haiku Journal, The Rotary Dial, Dappled Things, Main Street Rag, New Camaldoli Hermitage Newsletter, St. Katherine's Review, Ilya's Honey, Poydras Review, Euphony, St. Austin's Review,* and *Spirit & Life Magazine.*

Special thanks to Sr. Sarah Schwartzberg, OSB at *Spirit & Life,* all the anonymous Old and Middle English poets whose works glow but who will never be known by name, William Langland (for the model and so much more), and the great Vyāsa, whose world-embracing poem will never grow old. Also, deep gratitude to Mamie Riyeff, Paul Riyeff, and Chris Waters, without whose companionship thru the years these poems would never have been made.

Hæfe nu boc awritne bruca mið willa
symle mið soðum gileofa sibb is eghwæm leofost.

—Owun

n. *palmer*: 1. a pilgrim returning from the Holy Land with a palm frond; 2. any pilgrim; 3. someone who wanders idly

> And thou, desire, who art about to sing,
> sharpened by laughter and pleasure's sting,
> measure once more the space reserved for the irruption of song.
> The soul's claims on the flesh are extreme. May they keep us alert!
> And let some very powerful movement carry us to our limits,
> and beyond our limits.
> —Saint-John Perse, *Winds* (trans. Hugh Chisholm)

> The love which is beyond all feeling, the peace which is beyond all feeling,
> the joy which is beyond all feeling. Beyond love, peace, joy.
> A state of being beyond, in which we sink . . . What is it that sinks?
> I do not know, but there is a "sinking,"
> as when we say that we sink into sleep,
> sink into our mother's arms. A "surrender" of self,
> but a surrender to no one and to no thing, but just a surrender.

—from the spiritual diary of Swāmī Abhishiktānanda
July 17, 1952

Proœmium

Y shope me into shroudes as Y a shep were;
In abite as an heremite vnholy of werkes
Wente forth in the world wondres to here,
And say many selles and selkouthe thynges . . .
Me biful for to slepe, for werynesse ofwalked,
And in a launde as Y lay, lened Y and slepte,
And merueylousliche me mette, as Y may yow telle.

I shaped myself in shrouds a sheep to appear;
in a habit like a hermit unholy in works
forth I went in the world, wonders to hear,
and saw such sights and strange things . . .
Weary from walking, I went down to sleep,
and laying down in a new land I leant back and slept,
and I met marvelous dreams, as I may tell you now.

—*Piers Plowman C-Text,* Prologue 2-5, 7-9

1

AFTER NEZAHUALCOYOTL

> "Sweet-smelling flowers, precious flowers,
> with eagerness have I longed for them,
> empty wisdom had I."
> —*Nezahualcoyotl (Fastingcoyote)*

There are flowers to drown in
flowers that eyes
cannot see

> *Jade-tear flowers*
> *Diamond-sight flowers*

I will fill my mouth
with the frothing chocolate
flowers of ages
past and gone
I will sing with my mouth
full of their dark
and pungent fragrance

> *Kāvya flowers*
> *Piyyut flowers*

I come for visions
for dreams in water
the frothing chocolate
the honeyed chocolate
the spiced chocolate
flowing into the sun

> *Christ's-wounds flowers*
> *Dolorous-Passion flowers*

The senses, the night
are calling for the other
world, don't worry—
it won't take long
to find yourself there

                    Sapphire-crown flowers
                    Far-away flowers

I come for visions
for dreams in water
the frothing chocolate
the honeyed chocolate
the spiced chocolate
flowing into the sun

                    Burning-cacao flowers
                    Golden-dew flowers

Will there be more lives
to live here?
No, we see
but one life
we see the fading
flowers, the wilting
the red bird
dying in its plumes

                    Drowning flowers
                    Shānta flowers

I come for visions
for dreams in water
the frothing chocolate
the honeyed chocolate
the spiced chocolate
flowing into the sun

                    Emerald-water flowers
                    Far-and-near flowers
                    Precious flowers
                    Sweet-smelling flowers

Take up the flowers
inebriating flowers
the flowers in our hands
enjoy them as they fade

their fragrant corollas
calling to the sun

I. Vita

"Peter!" quod a plouhman, and potte forth his heued,
"I knowe hym as kyndely as clerk doth his bokes. . . .
Bothe to sowe and to sette the while Y swynke myhte
And to sowen his seed, suewen his bestes,
Withynne and withouten to wayten his profit. . . .
And hoso wilneth to wyte where that Treuthe woneth
Y wol wissen yow wel ryht to his place. . . .
Ac hoso wol wende ther Treuthe is, this is the way theder. . . ."

"By Peter!" said a ploughman, and put out his head,
"I know Truth as naturally as a scholar knows books. . . .
Both sowing and saving with sweat I labor,
sowing his seed and seeing to his beasts,
awaiting his profits both within and without. . . .
And whoever desires to discern where Truth dwells
I'll show you right sharp to his sure abode. . . ."

—*Piers Plowman C-Text,* VII 182-83, 186-88, 198-99, 205

BIRTH IMAGINED FROM A DIFFERENT ROOM

Milwaukee, WI

a full moon like Krishna's celestial discus
hangs white and luminous over the city—
awaiting the third living discharge to leap
from your contracting uterus.
outside, a nineteenth-century water tower
pines for the moon, and we see the city
thru plateglass, the lake's expanse
below brick spires, its glinting aquatic mansions
hiding slick and living treasures. I plan
unnecessary fund raisers as we wait, you misremember
me as my buddy Steve slicing open my thumb
down to the bone on a bluff over Devil's Lake—
though my morphine drip was really
after wild mushroom stromboli outside Big Sur,
careening down Highway 1 to San Simeon
for fluids and pain relief from doctors
I couldn't hear. and the dulcet strains
of Arcangelo Corelli spin delicate webs
around the room the tone of harpsichords
culled from a stop at St. Paul's in Minnesota
one damp summer morning a decade ago.
and you shake. and you breathe.
and soon I will meet this wet and
shining gem as he gasps his first gasp
here in the beautiful sad old world.

PENWITH

-for ancestors

We railed it from Holyhead to Birmingham,
sleeping splayed across three seats like vagrants,
a Welsh child crawling down luggage racks
to case us out, hills rolling by outside.
Eyelids like metal traps resisting peregrinations
but the world springs back to form and clarity
over trestles in mine-ruin Redruth,
downtown Camborne—and little did we suspect
ancestral hamlet Gwillanwarthas a stone's throw away.
Our uphill tramp along Penzance soaked cement
to the wrong hostel almost too much to take.
Back down petunia-lined lanes of thatched roofs—
who knew they still took the time?
Bags thrown on bunks that make you sad
how wet they are—we're told that's just Cornwall, mate—
and our clothes, our shoes did not dry for four days' time,
despite the hostel dryer's heroic and repeated attempts.
The rock, the seabirds too many to number and shades of difference,
another car cramped and rented, sitting in inverted seats,
but the same stick: we had that.
And you drove up the curb off Alverton Street
to the horror of several Cornish folk passing by
to their morning papers and pasties.
We kept the sea to our left on our circumambulation
always moving, the next fountain, the next cairn
and dolmen and churchyard, the next pond with
white streaks of swan and springs swallowed up
by time, padding up the A-30 to Bodmin Moor,
making wrong turns down claustrophobic lanes
to Lamorna Cove with housewives' sidelong glances
as they potted plants with strangers driving slowly past
and tossing off the world, the forest strange in these parts and sopping.
Why did we careen down backways, narrow and hard as rock
to find standing stone rings in farmers' fields,
searching miry paths hung with moss for baptistries

left standing since the Reformation? Why the restless
surge to moor and field and shore in damp and rain,
in hard grey midmornings and no food 'til teatime?
The cracked and bristling grass that welcomed our feet,
the draughts from Iron Age wells and flowering club moss?
How can we know? The last bleak stretch of path
down unknown woods, opening out into clearings
lined with mud and lichen, into centuries, then turning 'round,
was more than enough—circling Penwith into the dawn
of a metallic wind-swept eternity.

LIVING ALONE IN NORTH BAY

I fill a space in this rich present,
claiming each *taqueria* and lingerie

store as my own. We find happiness
as we can. Stumbling on choice, shouldering
personhood, sharing pain.

Maybe they don't see me, so many
still creatures off to ashes.
Only so many times to look

into seamless eyes, seeing a soul
wrapped neatly in its own mortality,
in shifting limbs and slow respiration.

TEA POEMS

I. *Dushanbe Tea House—Boulder, CO 2001*

The seats are strangely cool
    tonight, the tea is not:
its yellow-green mass
    coddled in white clay.
New sounds splash on the air,
    and still there's quiet inside.

II. *3rd Street and Highway 101—San Rafael, CA 2005*

Alone, I watch my step walking
a familiar street in San Rafael.

The air tonight is oolong tea—
glowing lights wrap me up
and tangled blankets shape the horizon.

The stars of evening shine and I
see them, knowing a moment's peace.

DINNER OUTSIDE TIME IN KILLARNEY

-for my brother

It was years before the housing market crashed,
    before our children were born:
leaving upper Midwest lands for the shores
    of Éire and greater Britain.
Cutting thru crisp morning from Dublin town
    to western Kerry and Ardmore.
And you drove that stick past rivers and castles—thru streams!
    —our mechanical pilgrimage.
Ireland's hardened saints of old, leaving
    home and hearth and all,
bathing neck-deep in icy streams
    on fire for another world,
would've been proud seeing your holy maneuvers
    faring in a strange land.
Our first night in Killarney of greenest green
    and the great empty cathedral,
whose meticulous landscaping staged brick and mortar
    against the setting sun.
A full day of driving, watching sun-streams wash
    across Cistercian ruins,
evading the cows and ruminating bulls who keep
    vigil here now,
carefully brooding where white-robed bees once hived—
    strange lay brothers.
And now for food; the only meal for two
    broke and hungry brothers
who came across the sea with too few
    Euros between them.
Atop a crest in Aghadoe, looking
    down on sapphire waters,
three tumbling peaks cut toward an island
    and we hear the care-free calls
of three unknown birds, the exhalations
    of one tawny horse.
And we decide in the dying light to find somewhere

to eat away down in town.
Thru streets, past hedges, under striped awnings
　　we spot an Indian place.
With little strength left we slink in the door,
　　greeted by side-long glances
from hostess, maître d', and waitress, the first
　　of whom mumbles something.
It becomes painfully obvious, without the words beings said,
　　you and I are not
the American tourists they want to see: disheveled,
　　stained second-hand clothes,
mismatched hats and shoes, unfortunate facial
　　hair and soiled backpacks—
not polished Southerners and New Englanders, tired from castle-
　　touring, but put together.
Without a classist word, the maître d' transports
　　us to the hungry street
to find other fare. And we find another
　　Indian restaurant
two blocks over—they see the hunger
　　in our faces and welcome us,
showing us to a corner table past high-contrast
　　prints of Krishna and Rādhā.
And there we feast for two hours: samosas,
　　papadums, curry,
chai with such spices, and we have to pour
　　the sharp, black infusion
into warmed, ceramic cups, add cool cream
　　and mountains of molassesed sugar.
We feast not to spite the other restaurant's
　　staff, no—we feast because
the verdant closeness of life had us there,
　　wrapped in its fecund embrace,
strangers moving from place to place for the sheer
　　joy of movement unrehearsed.
Now, years have passed: you wear loafers
　　and black-rimmed glasses,
our hair cut too short to make much fuss,

ties without irony.
But I imagine if that hostess and maître d'
    looked square in our eyes
today, they would still discreetly usher us out
    into the hungry street,
and we'd still be left to find our feast
    elsewhere—but together.

ON READING KEROUAC'S BIG SUR *AGAIN AFTER SIXTEEN YEARS*

Milwaukee, Lower East Side

St. John's day 2016 and the grey
salt-crusted streets of Milwaukee
welcome us home—a wife and two kids
in back, a third growing in the dark wet
of her womb. The biting cold funnels
between old multi-level houses split into
flats that Poles built nearly a century
ago. And opening a reissue of *Big Sur*
from Penguin raises phantoms
from youth, bearded ecstatic youth,
that hang thick just below the surface—
Chris, who suffers good-naturedly in his
flannel shirts, and Steve who went into
the Air Force, and Paul who loved sound
poetry and someone I won't name who
tried harder than most. And we had
the chance to be "real" bohemians then—
To rush headlong into the sullen drunken
madness Jack describes, as he hides
from all the sad mess of the world
that no one can speak to anymore—
And it's gone and getting bigger for sixty years.
There were visions and spontaneous campouts
in Boulder foothills—drumming and golden dreams
spread over our shoulders like hidden
green scapulars. A naïve thirst
for everything and a giddy call in the bones
suffocating for joy in the gone night,
driving for days to see acquaintances spread thru-out
the country, working on vegetable farms, sleeping
in Iowa campgrounds with the Great Blue Heron ruling over
the lazing river every beatific twilight—
But unlike Jack and his grim buddies,
most of us veered off course, kept ourselves

from the dark roses of the unborn—
And on this side of that Great Divide all-holy
we're hugging our Golden Eternity quietly in brief
moments between toddlers' incessant questions,
giant timeblocks of small hands and running,
and doing the next square thing. And maybe
Jack's with St. Michael right now, thinking,
"O, thank God!"—

INTERLUDE

It's springtime again, and my daughter
rolls on the floor, jabbering.

It's hot and being human
is still hard. The years

dividing moments can't
touch this. Not at all.

ON THE DEATHS OF TWO UNCLES IN WINTER

"And still the capsules of nothingness in our living mouths."
—*Saint-John Perse,* Winds *(trans. Hugh Chisholm)*

the river and a platform brick and concrete the color
of sand beneath grass five feet below the wall
that holds the schoolfield afloat over running water.
the eye drinks down the waterfall frozen eight feet
tall above the Centerway dam, horizon and warehouse,
a bowling alley, the spire of a Catholic church
the Irish built shooting out the trees like wire
from a torn cable left to waste away
in one of these ailing and empty gravel lots
breathing languor.

                  over on the west side of town
uncle Louis slipped into small comas
in the middle of words as clots passed into and out of
his German heart. and down on Jackson uncle Nick
didn't mind driving the getaway car for friends
and petty crimes. but that's all over now.
steel and combustion engines and sky. and the river
doesn't know. and the river doesn't mind.
and we go our way as it rolls in and out
of us, over mud and rusted fencing
down past the city limits out into the world.

SHORTS-I

A Fountain in Springtime

the sun slips out, sowing warmth.
a duck floats in the fountain, sleeping—
unaware of talk, too tired to bother.
a calm spring breeze blows through the water:
head in wing, watching dream.

Madison, 2009

The Thick of It

I sit smiling in a basement office
editing five centuries of psalter—
the world devouring my grateful heart.

haiku after three children

porridge in the pot
coffee in the silent mill
emptiness abounds

*

winter is coming
potage céline warms on stove
ah—*c'est magnifique!*

*

prone and sick in bed
window speaks a summer show'r
not all is suff'ring

Behind

Sometimes, time's hold evaporates
Sometimes, one sees straight through it

On cool evenings in mid-summer
the sun sets the sky ablaze, and the night

continues on, heavy with the scent
of flowers, leaving time behind

Autumn Gales

the seabirds watch and wait
they wait and watch some more
wind and water all they know
the seabirds watch and wait

ST. LEVAN'S WELL: A TRIOLET

St. Levan, Cornwall

We walked along a forest path
and drank from Selevan's well.
In drinking there we drank the past;
we walked along a forest path.
And though we knew it couldn't last
as the spring flowed down to the cliff-wrapped swell—
we walked along a forest path
and drank from Selevan's well.

WAY BACK-I

Proverbs of Chaucer
-From the Middle English

What to do with so many clothes
on such a hot summer's day?
After heat comes the cold:
no one should throw his coat away.

*

I cannot gather in these two arms
the expansive compass of this broad earth.
The one who wants too much of its forms
retains little of lasting worth.

Almsgiving
-From the Old English

That disciple is blest whose spirit burns
with generosity, renovating the inner room
of her heart. The world rejoices at her worthiness
and the Lord glories in the glow of her light.

Jesus ben Sirach says a surging
flame will be snuffed, raging fires
put down with welling water—no longer
able to damage dwellings with burning—
when that disciple douses sin, healing souls
with the gracious gift of her gladsome alms.

Nobility
-A Middle English Ballade by Geoffrey Chaucer

That first man, the source of nobility—
those who long on earth to be noble too
must follow his paths, guiding hand and eye
to virtue, ridding vice from all they do.
For worthiness ever longs for what is true,
for nothing less (as I have ever found),

although he wear a collar, suit, or crown.

This first of men was pure on every side:
true of his word, sober, kind, and free,
humble in spirit, always occupied
to ward off sloth and lust and vanity.
Unless his heir loves virtue and charity
he is not noble—nor his conscience sound—
although he wear a collar, suit, or crown.

Vice may well be heir to inheritance,
but no man can (as others plainly see)
grant his heirs his virtuous excellence
(that is no one's family pedigree
but that first father's, reposed in majesty,
who freely makes heirs of those his grace surrounds),
although he wear a collar, suit, or crown.

Truth
-A Middle English Ballade of Good Counsel by Geoffrey Chaucer

Flee the crowd and dwell securely in trueness.
Let your own suffice, though it not be much,
for greed leads to hate and grasping to coldness;
the crowd leads to envy, and wealth deceives such
as hold too tightly everything they touch.
Rule yourself well, that others clearly see,
and have no doubt: the truth shall set you free.

Don't try to amend all that is amiss,
trusting that Lady who spins like a ball;
true rest lies in spurning busyness.
There's no sense in kicking the point of an awl
nor in the crock's struggle against a wall.
Rule yourself, you who rule others' deeds,
and have no doubt: the truth shall set you free.

Take what is sent to you in obedience;
struggle, for this world surely begs a fall.
We have no home here, only wilderness.

Go forth, pilgrim! Go forth, beast, from your stall!
Know our true home and thank the God of all.
Hold your course and follow your spirit's lead,
and have no doubt: the truth shall set you free.

In Praise of Wine
-From the Middle English of John Lydgate, OSB

Wine, we praise your nine gracious virtues!
You comfort the heart, clear the weakened sight,
gladden the spirit with mirth we can't refuse.
You heat the temper with your subtle bite,
sharpen wits, and stoke courage in a fight.
You clean our wounds, refine our boorish state.
Wine, you provide our feasts with rubied light—
drunk in measure, you're virtue's very gate.

THE RELICS OF ST. ANTHONY'S TONGUE AND VOCAL CHORDS

Padua, Trinity Sunday 2008

Such a small selection
    of desiccated flesh—
swallowing time and eternity
    up.

SACCIDĀNANDA

*Woodbourne (near where my
great-grandfather David's cabin sat),
Catskill Mountains, 2003*

The morning sun begins to sing along
crowned treetops, growing dampness in the air

Flowers transformed, leaving perfect Brahmin fingers,
ladles of butter calling to the bowing moon

In my heart's hidden cavern I catch a glimpse
of Melchizedek, peaceful priest and king

drawing off thick-pulled draughts, pouring
Vedic connections, cradled in obscurity:

an oblation obliquely exploding heaven and earth,
melting forms, relieving tortured structures

On planks of wood wrapped in blankets,
we sat chanting and hoping away

VISIONS OF RAIN: A TRIPTYCH

"And the man, hard among men, in the crowd, catches
himself thinking of the lyme-grass on the sands. . . .
'Once, once I had a taste for living without sweetness,
but now the Rains . . .' (Life rises to the storms on the
wings of refusal.)"
—*Saint-John Perse, Rains (trans. Denis Devlin)*

I.

A lull at work, so I go to see the master arriving at Poet's Corner a church
doubling as mausoleum and museum for the greats of English past, sit
before the tomb. <Three in the afternoon.> Next I know the master him-
self walking slowly in my direction an alcove nearby alongside the tomb,
drinking a glass of water from elsewhere. —What is this, then? speaking
in Modern English helping me along. —I've come to ask you for a plan.
—Lions have problems of their own, shifting his weight from one keen
arm to the other, and turtles have hard shells. —Yes, I see, Geoffrey, but
I have come to be a poet, for I've failed on my own. —The sun comes up
every day, only to go down again. <Nothing.> —Sir, what does it mean to
see? leaning forward now beginning to betray a certain irritation. —My
mind is overwhelmed with implacable visions of rain. —What do these
visions reveal? —Madness is the answer, and the only one. How else can
the bride respond? Blood coming to cheeks, I plead: And *who* is the bride?
—I left for the court as a child, my friend, and here I lie in Westminster's
modern relic. What more to be said? With that he excused himself, me
smiling lamely to the other visitors passing by with mind set, avoiding
their down-turned museum faces.

II.

One somber day thirteen-hundred years ago, Æthelbald the Mercian
heard tell in his exile of Guthlac, holy man of Croyland. Braving miles of
liquid highway, he arrives at the auspicious island: a gray patch of land, a
gray blanket of water and grass, sky rolling out off-gray in all directions.
Jumping from his skiff, Æthelbald looks about, spies a bundle of rags and
hair. —Is there something you need? asks the bundle squatting, at peace,
against a gnarled bush. —I am in exile and would know how to win the

favor of both God and man. To reveal wisdom, Guthlac stands erect, removes his scraggy robe without a trace of guile, urinates freely on a rather large tuft of sedge growing nearby. And from that day, the heavens opened to Æthelbald, and he ruled the Mercians in prosperity for many years.

III.

—What is it you're looking for? asks Æthelthryth of Ely. <You can call her "Audrey" if you like.> Young Ælfgifu approaches hesitating, but determined her flinty voice replies, I've come because I'm going to die. —I see no way 'round it, the abbess explains under her wimple. —But what is to be done? Ælfgifu presses. Æthelthryth looks toward sisters sweeping the sanctuary, back at the anxious woman before her. —Drink the Golden Eternity, dear, all of it, not letting the young sister avert her eyes from the flame in her own.

NOCTURNE

Janesville, WI 2004

These days go by; they sink
like empty fields—and we
slough off burdens, intricately

rowed. Taking moments
as if they matter, because
they matter. Reaching with quiet

abandon to nurse at the gnawing
breast of the stammering Milky
Way—alone and intimate.

We eat the cool sinking
dark, make it a part
of ourselves—the cranes and us.

AD INVITATORIUM (PS 100)

> jubilate deo omnis terra
> servite domino in laetitia (Ps 99:2)

Seven times a day, O Lord,
we'll cry to you. With joy we'll come
before the Creator of heaven and earth.
Each morning, still clasped inside my head
from sleep, I'll ask you to open my lips.
When our children whine, when coffee spills
all over the floor and we scream at red lights:
we'll sing, "Indeed, how good is the Lord!"
no matter how good or bad we are.
Seven times a day, O Lord—
and once a night if we're lucky—we will
slip from other duties to hallow
time, and offer our everything to you.

BASCOM HILL

Madison, WI 2009

A fumbling rush of a smile pours out of me:
it's autumn atop our tired moraine.

Lagging, a poor creature with a salutary grin,
beams of sunshine breaking cold through smooth

November skies. Slanted wind blowing
voices; squirrels approaching over dying grass.

I watch the cars and pavement to the south,
gold leaves on grey sky, and pray

to be a fool, to have the weakness and frailty
needed to be poor and gentle, that I may

smile a true smile, meeting eyes
that pass me with awe.

SEPTEMBER ENDED

"the cnott is knit, which mai not ben unbound"
—*John Lydgate, OSB,* The Temple of Glas

That night I drove home from Madison,
taking Highway 14 instead of the interstate—
a moon hanging cool and distinct above row
after row after row of corn no one can eat.
I came from my friend's house where we
made pakoras and chanted the night away,
soothing our manly loneliness with song.
I didn't know if you'd come by, so I sat
alone in my parents' dark living room
watching a solitary flame and wondering
to myself and the empty room if I would risk
ruining our friendship that night—if you
would come by like you'd said you would.
I had heroic thoughts of fleeing the world
or finally going to seminary, but
I wanted to place my hand on your
naked hip so badly, I probably would
not have made a very good monk.
And I heard you knock on the front door,
standing blushing in the moonlight
having just left a party around
the block. I invited you in as I had
so many times before. And though no clothes
were removed and nothing was regretted,
though all we did was talk heated in the dark,
our fingers finding one another like curious
birds in the dim light upon a plaid couch,
that restraint sealed our fate in a way
I'd never known or expected,
and I awoke holding my best friend
close—loving the bleary shock.

ON READING VYĀSA'S MAHĀBHĀRATA ON LAKE MENDOTA

The blue-grey lake reflects the blue-grey sky,
and the quays jut out nearly forming a square.
This crumbling ledge sings with the rolling clouds,
the waves and breeze making perfect choirs.

Warm hands and quiet thoughts pour from my mouth.

AGARIC

South Bend, IN 2014

You grow in sandy soil,
my eager hand plucked you.

No matter: your spore-load
has already dropped from

your tiny amber cap,
bell-shaped. Your smell

reminds me of dreams
and years that won't talk back.

The rains have come, washing
the earth, and you sing out

to fir trees and grass
blades, lazy dogs getting wet.

ON LAYING AWAKE ALL NIGHT

A field near Chicago, IL 2015

Planes fly cock-eyed over the tent,
punctuating my all-night vigil
under stars, Venus, the Big Dipper
I showed my daughter earlier tonight
with dark finger against dark sky.
My son barely breathes, dew point
dropping, like the gibbous moon over circling
trees—no sleep tonight, deep breaths
behind sealed eyelids, releasing the knots
in shoulder, hip, tongue, and brow.
Hours extend deep in the night,
into morning, the subtle shift of air
brings blood to my skin's covered surface
and no thought. A lone bird's
call in the pre-dawn stillness:
we two, waiting for the sun and day.
Twenty minutes later, a tanager
sings three notes, hesitates,
and then—starting here and there—
in the resting fields and patient trees,
thru-out the green-crowned sanctuary:
a full-throated avian chorus
reaching canticle out in all
directions, encompassing our camp in song.
And here is our matins' final note—
rising and falling, great and glorious.

MORTEM COTIDIE ANTE OCULOS

Rule of St. Benedict, 4:47

One day—who knows when—
I'll have no more chances to sit
on this concrete wall overlooking
the Rock River's lulling brown current.
I will be gone from the world.

We all need a place like that,
I suppose—a place where you go
and someday you will no longer
go there. And as you sit you think,
"I will be gone from the world."

MY EMBERING, ADVENT 2016

"Fasting days and emberings be
Lent, Whitsun, Holyrood and Lucie."
—popular English rhyme?

In late fall of 1961
or thereabouts, Annibale Bugnini—
suspected Freemason, eventual archbishop—
decided to do away with the Roman Calendar's
Quatuor Tempora. Sleep still in his eyes,
drinking his morning coffee, looking out
the window on St. Peter's, a child ran down
through the colonnade, raising pigeons
into the sky with no more than a voice,
and, as he tripped and fell down on the damp
Baroque cobblestones, the Roman grit,
our eventual archbishop determined in his heart
there would be no more of this Embertide.

                           Perhaps
if he had been a good Englishman
emberings would still be around, still
have haunted his musings, searching out, displacing
the Jewish and pagan touch of time and harvest,
celebrating and baptizing—Gregory said so, so...

But Bugnini didn't see the point, stripped
the calendar of centuries' four times a year
to step back, to celebrate four given
seasons, to fast and repent as prophets have done
and begged the crowds to do so long, so long.

I'm no Traditionalist, but on my walk to the bus
this morning in the dire cold off Lake Michigan,
snow and ice framing booted footsteps,
I determined to keep my embering:
a fornicator, liar, a gossip through and through,
a drunk and a gambler, slothful—an idolater!
I need an extra day or three to fast, to repent.

And so this sad year I'll keep my embering,
regardless of what anyone's rubrics say.

GOD LIVES ON THE LOWER EAST SIDE

anantalokāptim atho pratiṣṭhāṁviddhi, tvam etaṁ nihitaṁ guhāyām
—*Katha Upanishad*, 1.14

The snow atop St. Hedwig's
is a beacon splitting the sky—
winter on Brady Street.
Beneath the bell tower:
Polish stained glass,
a hundred years of hand oil
on polished pew backs,
and Body and Blood burning
beneath red candlelight.

Who awakens to the Spirit
but Christ himself dwelling
in the cave of the disciple's heart?
And what better way to sneak
him there, past intellect,
suspicion, judgment, good sense,
than swallowing bread and wine,
smuggling the Word made flesh
past brain and mouth into belly—
down into the cave of the heart
where lives nothing but Trinitarian
life—welling up
like the waters on the first day?

SO LET ME GRAZE

Your words worlds of flame
resting on the damp of your lip,
your scent the clouds passing by

So let me graze silently
past your tongue and teeth,
sunk down into your silence

II. Visio

Thenne Y afraynede at Fayth what al that fare bymente
And ho sholde iouste in Iersualem. "Iesus," he saide,
"And feche that the fende claymeth, Pers fruyt the plouhman. . . .
Liberum-dei-arbitrium *for loue hath vndertake*
That this Iesus of his gentrice shal iouste in Pers armes,
In his helm and in his haberion, humana natura;
That Crist be nat yknowe for consummatus deus,
In Pers plates the plouhman this prikiare shal ryde
For no dynt shal hym dere as in dietate patris."

Then I asked Faith what this flurry of activity foretold
and who would joust in Jerusalem. "Jesus," he said,
"fetching what the fiend claims, the fruit of Piers the Ploughman. . . .
The free-will-of-God out of love has willed
that Jesus will joust gently in Piers's arms,
in his helmet and hauberk, human-nature;
since Christ won't be seen for supreme-God,
in Piers's plated armor this pricker will ride,
for no hit can harm him in-the-Father's-divinity."

—*Piers Plowman C-Text*, XX 16-19, 21-25

41

A PROPOSITION

dry the gourd
remove its seeds
weigh the waters
by measure

the moon is hanging
big and wide
over Milwaukee

spreading waves
through the clouds over
Lake Michigan

embrace me longer
than is comfortable

tonight all things
end tonight
we will see
where dreams go

meet me on the curving
path leading down
to the frozen river

look me in the eye
and say we'll live
only as long
as necessary

I won't mind how
we get down there
as long as your
falling hair gets
into my mouth

and I can lose track
of where you are
as the lights pour

all around me
as the lights pour
all around me

SHORTS-II

Peruvianus

Making love to February air,
staring out at neon lights freezing
Droning into a rising sun
and drinking soma in the mind—
this beatific brace stunts every thought
settling simply with a longing laugh.

Morcella: A Fragment

Late April, and morels are in the land—
you *know* morels are in the land by the smell
Birds turn their bodies into verdant fans—
everyday more of their exhibitionist display
This foray my meager but exalted *non serviam*
Lilac. Squirrel ear. Standing Elm.

IMAGES FOR HADEWIJCH OF BRABANT

I. *Spring Brook—Janesville, WI*

still haunches. grey coat.
small movements of curled tail
take in every contour of every
blade of grass
as minute mammalian lungs
fill with air, empty.
do not dart. do not stir
too hastily.
he'll come right up to you
if you wait—if you try to snatch him:
there you are.

II. *Durward's Glen—Baraboo, WI*

the water pours but never leaves:
from fullness only fullness,
as the Upanishad says.
cupped hands and wet hair,
face, falling pine cones overhead—
and the spring will not stop.

III. *Lower East Side—Milwaukee, WI*

dark streets, dawn,
long shadows. saturated light
falls on the gable across the street.
if this is not bliss?
no frog, no elderberry.

FOUR SAPPHIRES

"Sinking in your shipwreck,
I will never rest until I've reached
the very bottom of your heart—
'til I am sheltered there!"

> —*Swāmī Abhishīktananda's rendering of a stanza from Shrī Ramana Maharshi's "Marital Garland of Letters," addressed to the holy mountain Arunāchala (trans. Jacob Riyeff)*

I.

You've been unfair,
O Arunāchala,
leaving me here
to sit alone
in your valley,
a spurned lover
crying in the heavy
air underneath
his blanket

II.

Make me the tea
pouring down
the sides of your porcelain
cup as you drink
too fast and greedily,
wetting your beard
and dripping onto
your chest

III.

I am fruit
newly picked
and ripe, the scent
stirring something
in your limbs and belly

at once

IV.

Strip me, delight
in me, shower
me with yourself
as I come to see
in your grace that you
are me

SHĀNTIVANAM

For Swāmī Abhishiktānanda (Dom Henri Le Saux, OSB)
Et . . . invenissent eum trans mare (Jn 6:25)

We drove: damp forests, arid grasslands,
bluffside caves shaping our circuit,
noxious billboards swallowing air and sky.
St. Stephen's day and silence and Vespers
with strangers, the Forest of Peace, West.
And there on the low bookcase are tomes,
not water damaged, but not preserved, a pleasant
mustiness rising to greet olfactory organs among
the yellowed pages—and, my God, who *is* this?

He says, "*saccidānanda*," and grins.
From the winds of Gangotri he begins
his descent: a Breton with stars crowding
his teeth, hair abrupt and spangled:
a scarlet howler, a candle snuffed—
I lie in darkness below the pine canopy
thousands of miles from your grave,
a sly smile a signal of homecoming—
there is no Abhishik. And all
that's left from this is the Father.

WAY BACK-II

I Ought to Weep
-From a Middle English poem of the early 14th century

When I see the Lord
on the cross above,
my lover having suffered
tortures enough—
his back scourged,
his side pierced,
and all for love—
well ought I to weep
and Christ's commandments keep:
if I know aught of love,
if I know aught of love,
if I know aught of love.

What Reason Reason Give?
*-An updating of a 16th-century poem scribbled into the record book of the
Benedictine Abbey of St. Albans in England*

A god and yet a man,
a maid and yet a mother—
the mind wonders as it can,
conceiving something or other.

A god, and can he die?
A dead man—can he live?
What can the mind reply?
What reason reason give?

God and Mother Church teach it.
Our minds sink, too far under
in reason's power to reach it.
Believe, and leave off to wonder.

Adam Laid in Bondage
-From a Middle English poem of the 15th century

Adam laid in bondage,
bound in many bonds:
four thousand winters
didn't seem too long.
All for the fruit it was,
the perilous fruit he took,
so the wise ones tell us
is written in God's Book.

Though, had he the fruit not taken,
the fruit not been taken,
nor would ever our Lady
have become the Queen of Heaven.
Blessed be the moment
he took that fruit, because
now we can gladly sing,
"*Deo gratias*!

Grieving for Mary
-From a Middle English poem of the early 13th century

Her son approaches the skullish place—
I grieve, Mary, when I see your face.
Upon the cross her Son is hung—
I grieve, Mary, for you and your Son.

The Child Jesus to Mary, the Rose
-A Middle English Ballade by John Lydgate, OSB

My Father, seeing your hopeful meekness,
spread balm like dew on Roses where you stood
and sent his Spirit, summit of cleanness,
into your breast (O Rose of womanhood!)
when I for man was born in humble manhood:
for this, with Roses of heavenly sway,
I rejoice to play before your face.

Kindest mother! who from the first enclosed
the blesséd bud that sprang out of Jesse,
of Judah you're the single perfect Rose
the Father chose for your humility—
you the purest, never fading, bore me:
for this, with myriad Roses pure and chaste,
I rejoice to play before your face.

O mother! mother! in mercy you stand,
fairest mother living on whom we call!
Though I have suffered bloody wounds for man,
behold, five Roses there among them all
against whose mercies devils fight and fall.
Rose of succor, hear man's surest grace:
when to me they pray before your face.

Gold and the World's Fine Pleasures
-From a Middle English poem of the 14th century

Gold and the world's fine pleasures
are dust before Christ's cross.
Would I were clothed in the finest treasure,
his blood beyond all cost,
and gone to his heart that takes mine in
where there is the richest food:
then I'd care not for family and kin,
for there is every good.

IN HIEZECHIHELEM

Gregory told us how it is.
Around us a single voice: relentless,
limiting the bones, the joints, the very
brain. Lurching and crushed and caught.

A multitude of voices urges us onward:
calling now and calling then,
skirting edges and freeing time.

From us a single voice: relentless,
ripping and tearing with loving echoes,
while here is all our echoes know.
Gregory told us how it is.

MORE TEA

If anyone thinks that drinking tea
is simply drinking tea,
let us feel sorry for him.

I know that our heads will break
and the ghosts of all anyone ever knew
will soar back and forth
between us—

Once you've filled your mouth with
inappropriate draughts
and the theanine has gone to your head
and heart,
kiss my forehead and get up—
call for more tea.

SUMMER LINGERS: A MODIFIED RONDEAU

Hot days like this one wonders:
    hot days in autumn, listless.
        One wonders why one's maker
        made one as one is—
    on days with time to wonder.

Hot days to lose one struggles:
autumn days with naught to do.
Made by one's brilliant maker—
    hot days like this.

Foggy days in restive duty,
    hazy days in crumbling hours:
        one looks askance for solace,
        too tired to fall, to reel.
    Static days of open numbness—
    hot days like this.

DE ISAAC

When Isaac took Rebekah into his tent
a world was born for love, for grandeur, and, finally,

death. As a lover kissing lover's softest thighs—
this is how we will love each other—as one
on fire tasting mellowed fruits. So sing

my voice, if you can, sing a song of love
like Isaac's—a love so close it can't but sear.

AFTER HAFIZ

> "Love sometimes gets tired of speaking sweetly
> and wants to rip to shreds
> all your erroneous notions of truth"
>> —*Hafiz, "Tired of Speaking Sweetly" (trans. Daniel Ladinsky)*

God is a five-month old—
his spit-up flowing down
the back of your leg his grace
as you read him the poems of Hafiz

Now he's waiting in the other
room for you to play
He's smiling slow and wide

A WEDDING SONG

Ab illo benedicaris
in cuius honorem cremaberis

I. *Proem*

Spent sorrows say too much—
recollections and losses dispersed
and spread in shameful, shallow choices,
scraping streambeds, forest floors,
confusing love and holding hands—
but I look back, calm and burdened,
telling of love long-delayed
and thinking on the finality I saw gnaw
your fears as you held peonies fine
and clouding, smelling sweet from your hands
before the wedding feast began.

II. *Pueritia*

I see Midwest playgrounds, grass
alive with everything and green oaks—
friends that said farewell in their way—
and always I was looking for you.
When cheap smoke searched my lungs
and boyish hapless perversions
moved through my limbs, lunging at grace,
looming and yearning and left in basements,
in the waters of the quiet sand quarry
that filled in eighty years ago,
mistaking young faces for friendship,
grasping hands and seeking grace
in the loose soil of Atlas Pit.
All moving, mingling with my cries
at dawn and help I left behind.
From fullness comes fullness and I chased that vision,
that glorious meeting I meant to describe.

III. *Visio*

The earth sang under desert stars,
a breaking open of my ailing head
on a sad basement floor in December.
A light shone and dimmed, disappearing,
and always it was glowing alive in the mind.
The world opened a blossom to the eye
and I mistook her glory for God:
great tryptamine visions trailed
wreathes of smoke in Colorado
twilights—plants teaching tangled lessons.
And all the night-visions, valleys,
and mountains, the pujas with their eager offerings,
all the talk in Persian tea-houses
and all the tea in all the world
couldn't answer my heart's ailing.

IV. *Discrimen et Thea*

Bitter combinings in clear cups
expanded out to unknowable love:
that awful darkness that clouds the approach
of our luminous moments, our intimate turns.
Coffee hits like a cold hammer,
but tea's not-two comes on like sainthood.
I headed your way and met Heaven's Queen
without knowing either as the longing eye turned.

V. *Nuptiae*

I see you that morning when a man was ready—
flesh and flesh—flesh all-holy!
We recalled the keen redemption
of mortal flesh, merged in coitus,
a mirror of Love Who Is.
Movement satisfies, but never enough:
power is not enough, not power
nor unknowability, knotted crowds

pouring effortlessly into that mystery
I wish I could tell. We've left here,
joint-bonds unloosed, illumined now:
this big-red-robe pouring
steam and delicate aromas, song
that crushes the heart, yawning and crying
that all is well but not well—and these
are not-two, and we yearn. We yearn. We yearn,
and yet not one thing within
our humble compass is near enough:
not strength or devotion, not life or death,
not me and not you and not bodies or minds—
Love alone can drag us along
and this tumbling satire finds rest and solace
in the bones and the skin in the arc of your arms.

LET'S PLAY: A MIRROR SONNET

And here I am, panting in the darkness again—
sunk past becoming, drawn to one in three,
three in one. Left here with only my pain,
like when a teenage love says "we'll see,"
followed up by "don't call anymore."
A razorblade to the flesh, curling blood
out onto bills strewn on the floor,
jilted and happy to see the life that was cut.
Your not-two is some kind of game, sunk
into *shunyata*'s zero—one and another, alone—
what the hell's the difference, it's never enough.
Lying here, there, naked as a stone.
And all I want in life is more of you—
kiss me and don't you dare say there are two.
Kiss me and don't you dare say there are two.
and all I want in life is more of you—
laying here, there, naked as a stone.
What the hell's the difference? it's never enough.
Into *shunyata*'s zero—one and another, alone—
your not-two is some kind of game, sunk,
jilted and happy to see the life that was cut
out onto bills strewn on the floor,
a razorblade to the flesh, curling blood,
followed up by "don't call anymore,"
like when a teenage love says, "we'll see."
Three in one, left here with only my pain
sunk past becoming, drawn to one in three.
And here I am, panting in the darkness again.

Postludus

"By Crist," quod Consience tho, "Y wol bicome a pilgrime
And wenden as wyde as the world renneth
To seke Peres the plouhman, that Pruyde myhte destruye. . . .
Now Kynde me avenge,
And sende me hap and hele til Y haue Peres plouhman."
And sethe he gradde aftur Grace tyl Y gan awake.

"By Christ," Conscience said, "I will become a pilgrim
and wander as wide as the world extends
to seek Piers the Plowman, who might destroy Pride. . . .
Now Nature, right my wrongs,
and send me profit and health 'til I have Piers the Plowman."
Then he groaned after Grace 'til I began to awake.

—*Piers Plowman C-Text*, XXII 380-82, 384-86

AFTER YOGEŚVARA

"with crabs and blooming moss and muddy water
and the sodden earth raised up by earthworms pushing
up from below;
these water-hollowed shorelands of the swampy streams
have set a mark upon my heart."

— *Yogeśvara, from Vidyākara's* Treasury *(trans. Daniel Ingalls)*

I.

A night of rain, and still the dampness in morning
air—gusts of wind and grayish light
as buses sprint down our boulevard.
We can see the moisture clinging to each
and every building—the pools of sand turned
to silty mud—hear the echoing calls
of three species of gull as they shout from the library's
roof. What is the discouraged scholar to do?

II.

The corolla of the gloaming sky
opens out to night—
its stamens every cold
mountain and dark-spangled tree,
its pistil the moon reigning
over all. Gracious
winds spread your
pollen throughout the abyss.

Sources Cited

Hafiz. *The Gift*. Translated by Daniel Ladinsky. New York: Penguin, 1999.

Langland, William. *Piers Plowman: A New Annotated Edition of the C-text*. Edited by Derek Pearsall. Exeter: University of Exeter Press, 2008.

Léon-Portilla, Miguel, ed. *Native Mesoamerican Spirituality: Ancient Myths, Discourses, Stories, Doctrines, Hymns, Poems from the Aztec, Yucatec, Quiche-Maya and Other Sacred Traditions*. Mahwah, NJ: Paulist Press, 1980.

Lydgate, John. *Temple of Glas*. Edited by J. Allan Mitchell. Kalamazoo, MI: Medieval Institute Publications, 2007.

Perse, Saint-John. *Collected Poems*. Princeton: Princeton University Press, 1983.

Swāmī Abhishiktānanda. *Ascent to the Depth of the Heart: The Spiritual Diary (1948-1973) of Swāmī Abhishiktānanda (Dom H. Le Saux)*. Edited by Raimon Panikkar and translated by David Fleming and James Stuart. Delhi: ISPCK, 1998.

———. *In the Bosom of the Father: The Collected Poems of a Benedictine Mystic*. Translated by Jacob Riyeff. Eugene, OR: Resource Publications, 2018.

Vidyākara. *Sanskrit Poetry*. Translated by Daniel H. H. Ingalls. Cambridge: Harvard University Press, 2000.

9 781532 662454